Designed by Flowerpot Press in Franklin, TN.
www.FlowerpotPress.com
Designer: Stephanie Meyers
Editor: Johannah Gilman Paiva
PAB-0808-0139
ISBN: 978-1-4867-0832-1
Made in China/Fabriqué en Chine

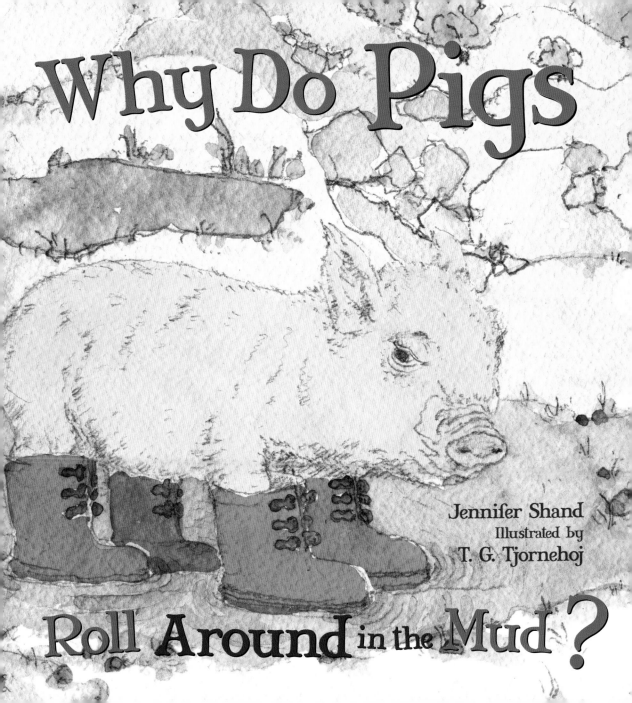

Why Do Pigs

Jennifer Shand
Illustrated by
T. G. Tjornehoj

Roll Around in the Mud?

How are farm animals specially made to
live on a farm? They have the farmer to
help take care of them, but they are on their
own most of the time. Each animal
must have something special about
them to live there.

Why do PIGS roll around in the MUD?

Is it because they just like being DIRTY?

Pigs do not have sweat
glands, so they roll around in
the mud to stay cool. The mud
also works like sunscreen and
bug spray—it helps keep the hot
sun and bugs off of them.

Why do DUCKS not mind being out in the RAIN?

Is it because they like to PLAY and SING in the rain?

No, that's silly!

Ducks don't mind being out in the
rain because their feathers are
waterproof! Ducks have a special oil
they spread on their feathers to help
keep them warm and dry.

Why do DONKEYS have such LONG EARS?

Is it to be able to wear big SUNGLASSES?

No, that's silly!

Donkeys have long
ears to help them hear
everything on the farm!
Donkeys are slower
than other
animals and
cautious, (some
people even say
stubborn), so being
able to hear things
that are far away
helps them know when
to get a running start!

Why do some COWS stand all day and some lie down?

Is it because the ones who are lying down are
SLEEPY and taking NAPS?

No, that's silly!

Cows lie down on the ground
when they are cold to help stay warm.
Cows stand up when they are hot because
air on their skin helps them cool down.

Why do CHICKENS dig themselves into the DIRT?

Is it because they are playing HIDE and SEEK
with their friends?

No, that's silly!

Chickens dig in the dirt because that's how they take a bath! The dirt absorbs grimy oil and helps get rid of little bugs that bite!

The animals on the farm sometimes do funny things or have funny features, but they are all for a good reason. Each funny thing they do or funny feature they have will help them live a longer and happier life on the farm!